AMAZING WINTER OLYMPICS

SNOWBOARDING

BY ASHLEY GISH

CREATIVE EDUCATION
CREATIVE PAPERBACKS

Published by Creative Education and Creative Paperbacks
P.O. Box 227, Mankato, Minnesota 56002
Creative Education and Creative Paperbacks are imprints of
The Creative Company
www.thecreativecompany.us

Design by The Design Lab
Production by Rachel Klimpel
Art direction by Rita Marshall
Printed in the United States of America

Photographs by Alamy (ITAR-TASS News Agency, Taka Wu, ZUMA
Press), AP Images (ASSOCIATED PRESS), Getty Images (Sam Mel-
lish/In Pictures, JAVIER SORIANO/AFP, Cameron Spencer/Getty
Images Sport), iStockphoto (AlexLMX, ultramarinfoto), Shutterstock
(FabrikaSimf, mountainpix, steba, yakub88, Leonard Zhukovsky)

Library of Congress Cataloging-in-Publication Data
Names: Gish, Ashley, author.
Title: Snowboarding / Ashley Gish.
Series: Amazing Winter Olympics.
Includes bibliographical references and index.
Summary: Celebrate the Winter Games with this high-interest
introduction to snowboarding, the sport known for its halfpipe and
slopestyle events. Also included is a biographical story about skier
and snowboarder Ester Ledecká.

Identifiers:
ISBN 978-1-64026-498-4 (hardcover)
ISBN 978-1-68277-050-4 (pbk)
ISBN 978-1-64000-628-7 (eBook)
This title has been submitted for CIP processing under LCCN
2021938159.

Table of Contents

Snowboarding

became popular in the 1970s. The first snowboards were made from wooden planks. Snowboard makers improved the boards. In 1998, the sport was added to the Winter Olympics. Competitors from Canada, France, Germany, and Switzerland won gold medals that year.

American Ross Powers won bronze at the 1998 Games in Nagano, Japan.

Snowboarding is

an exciting winter sport. Some snowboarders speed through a bumpy course or take big jumps. Other events include highflying tricks.

Snowboarding combines elements of surfing and skateboarding.

A helmet keeps the snowboarder's head safe and helps the ears stay warm and dry.

Snowboarders

wear warm jackets, snow pants, gloves, and helmets. Goggles protect their eyes. **Sponsor** logos are often printed on their clothing.

sponsor a person or company that pays for an athlete's equipment or gear

Snowboard boots have more ankle support than regular boots, and they are made to fit into bindings.

binding

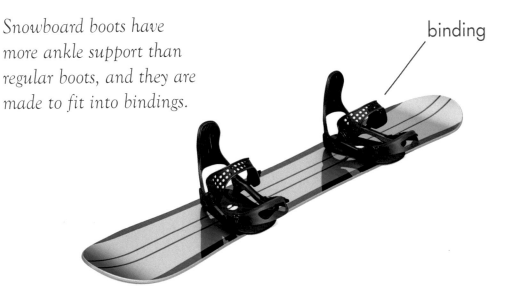

Modern boards are made of sleek **fiberglass**. Most are about 5 feet (1.5 m) long and 10 inches (25.4 cm) wide. The bottoms are waxed. This helps them glide on the snow. Bindings secure snowboarders' feet to the boards.

fiberglass a strong material made from a mix of glass and plastic fibers

Events include categories for men and women. In the halfpipe, snowboarders cruise up and down the sides of a U-shaped track. They do tricks and flips in the air. They earn points for creativity and control.

Athletes sometimes practice their tricks by landing on giant airbags set up near the halfpipe.

In the slopestyle event, athletes use jumps and rails to do tricks on the course.

Big air and slopestyle events send racers down a course with jumps. Snowboarders gain plenty of **amplitude**. Then they do tricks in the air.

amplitude air, or height, achieved from a jump

Snowboard cross racers must keep control and avoid hitting things to stay ahead of the others.

Parallel giant slalom racers

reach speeds of up to 43 miles (69.2 km) per hour. In this event, two athletes race side by side. During snowboard cross, athletes race in groups of four. They hit jumps and bumps. They fly through the air. The whole race is over in just a few minutes.

parallel lined up next to each other

slalom a downhill race over a winding or zigzag course marked by gates (flexible poles)

Shaun White became famous for skateboarding and snowboarding.

Shaun White is a legendary snowboarder. He brought new skills and tricks to the sport. He won Olympic gold medals in 2006, 2010, and 2018.

Snowboarding is

fun to watch. Catch the action during the next Winter Olympics as the world's top snowboarders display their amazing skills.

Riding a surface other than snow, like a rail, is called "jibbing."

Competitor Spotlight: Ester Ledecká

Ester Ledecká (*lih-DETS-ka*) is a skier and snowboarder from the Czech Republic. She is the first person to win gold medals in two different sports at the same Winter Games. She won gold in the alpine skiing super-G at the 2018 Games in Pyeongchang, South Korea. Days later, Ester raced to a gold-medal finish in the parallel giant slalom. She won gold again in that event at the 2022 Winter Olympics.

Read More

Chandler, Matt. *Chloe Kim*. Mankato, Minn.: Capstone, 2020.

McKinney, Donna B. *STEM in Snowboarding*. Minneapolis: Abdo, 2018.

Waxman, Laura Hamilton. *Snowboarding*. North Mankato, Minn.: Amicus, 2018.

Websites

Ester Ledecká: the Olympic Snowboarder Who Stunned the Ski World
https://www.youtube.com/watch?v=-4xlcz1t0zQ
Watch Ester Ledecká make Olympic history in Pyeongchang.

Shaun White: the Guy Who Raised the Bar in Snowboarding
https://www.youtube.com/watch?v=fqdAhD0CJqw
Learn more about Shaun White's incredible career.

Note: Every effort has been made to ensure that the websites listed above are suitable for children, that they have educational value, and that they contain no inappropriate material. However, because of the nature of the Internet, it is impossible to guarantee that these sites will remain active indefinitely or that their contents will not be altered.

Index